Creative Keyboard Presents

Hymns
Made Easy
for Piano
Book 1

arranged by Gail Smith

GW00385414

CHECK OUT CREATIVE KEYBOARD'S *FREE WEBZINE* @ www.creativekeyboard.com

Creative Keyboard Publications — MEL BAY

1 2 3 4 5 6 7 8 9 0

Table of Contents

O For a Thousand Tongues to Sing

Charles Wesley

Lowell Mason
arranged by Gail Smith

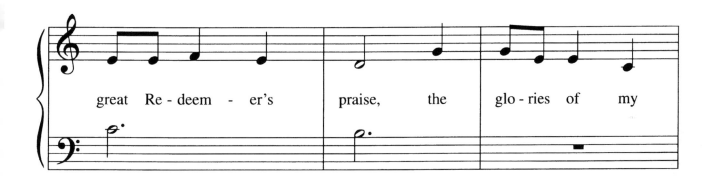

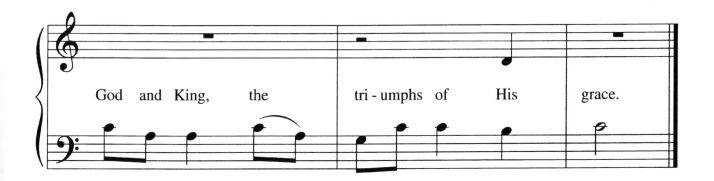

Blest Be the Tie that Binds

John Fawcett

Lowell Mason
arranged by Gail Smith

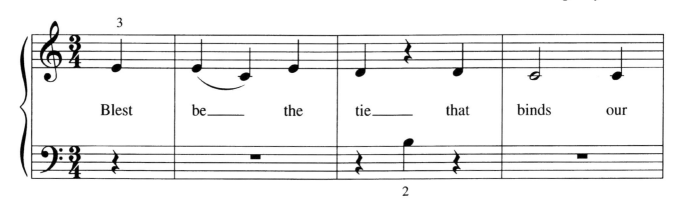

Blest be___ the tie___ that binds our

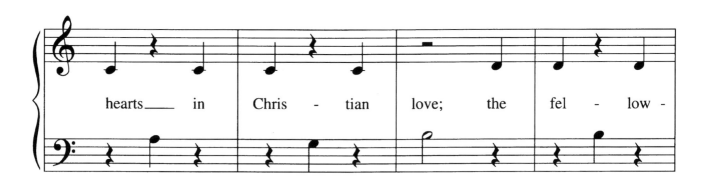

hearts___ in Chris - tian love; the fel - low -

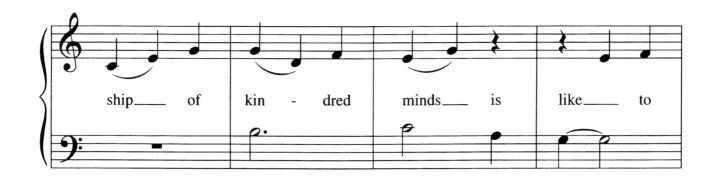

ship___ of kin - dred minds___ is like___ to

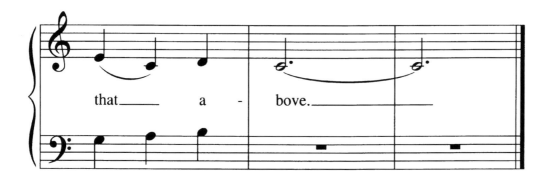

that___ a - bove.___

Doxology
Dedicated to Erika Hall

Thomas Ken

Louis Bourgeois
arranged by Gail Smith

Praise God from whom all bless - ings flow; Praise

Him, all crea - tures here be - low; Praise Him a - bove, ye

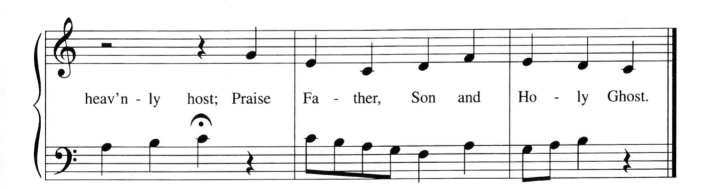

heav'n - ly host; Praise Fa - ther, Son and Ho - ly Ghost.

When I Survey the Wond'rous Cross

Isaac Watts

Lowell Mason
arranged by Gail Smith

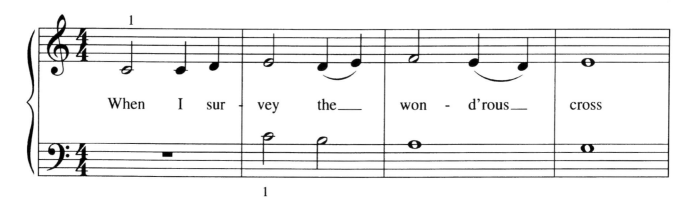

When I sur - vey the___ won - d'rous___ cross

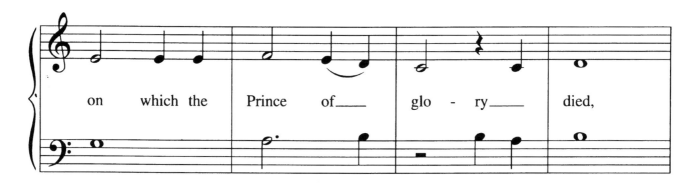

on which the Prince of___ glo - ry___ died,

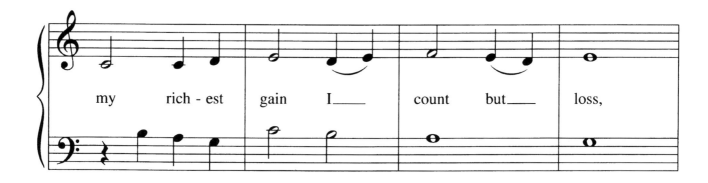

my rich - est gain I___ count but___ loss,

and pour con - tempt on all my___ pride.

6

Joyful, Joyful, We Adore Thee

Dedicated to Alex Hall

Henry Van Dyke

Beethoven
arranged by Gail Smith

Joy-ful, joy-ful, we a-dore Thee, God of glo-ry, Lord of love;

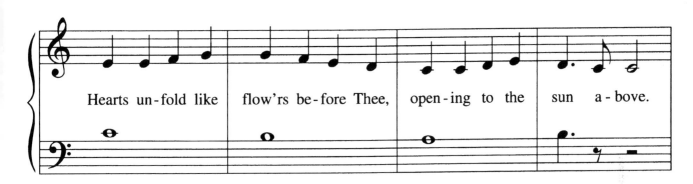

Hearts un-fold like flow'rs be-fore Thee, open-ing to the sun a-bove.

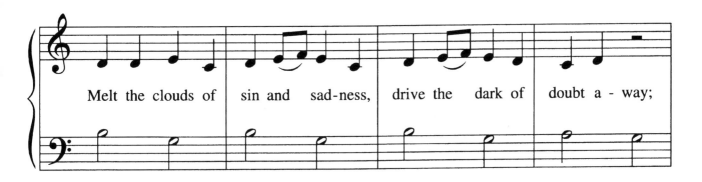

Melt the clouds of sin and sad-ness, drive the dark of doubt a-way;

Giv-er of im - mor-tal glad-ness, fill us with the light of day.

7

Jesus Loves Me
Dedicated to Alex Downs

Anna B. Warner

William Bradbury
arranged by Gail Smith

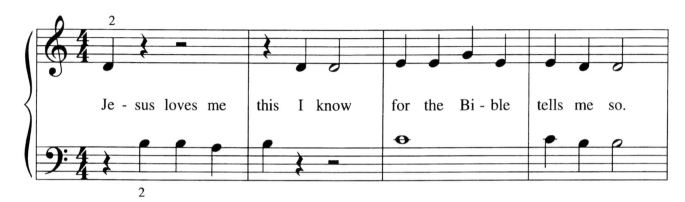

Je - sus loves me this I know for the Bi - ble tells me so.

Lit - tle ones to Him be - long, they are weak but He is strong.

Yes, Je - sus loves me. Yes, Je - sus loves me.

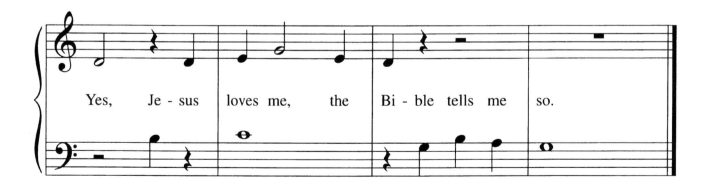

Yes, Je - sus loves me, the Bi - ble tells me so.

For the Beauty of the Earth

Dedicated to Elisabeth Marie Crane

Folliott S. Pierpoint

William H. Monk
arranged by Gail Smith

For the — beau - ty of the earth, for the glo - ry

of the skies, for the — love which from our birth

o - ver and a - round us lies: Lord of all, to

Thee we raise this our hymn of grate - ful praise.

Amazing Grace
Dedicated to Greta Anne Worden

John Newton

Traditional American Melody
arranged by Gail Smith

A - maz - ing ___ grace! How sweet the

sound that saved a ___ wretch like me! I

once ___ was ___ lost but now ___ am ___ found, was

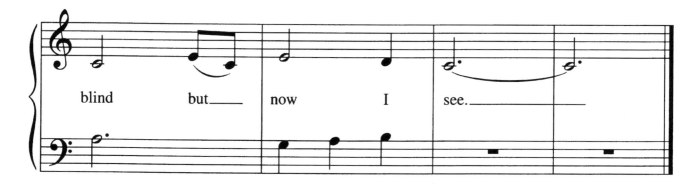

blind but ___ now I see. ___

O God, Our Help in Ages Past

Isaac Watts

William Croft
arranged by Gail Smith

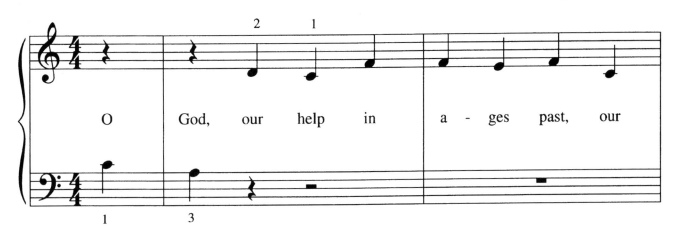

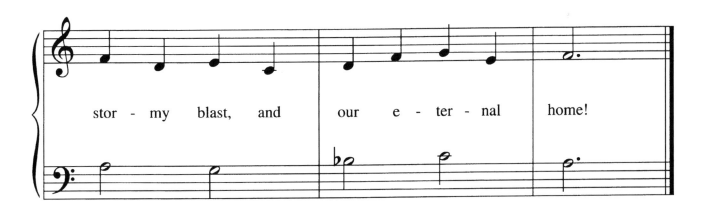

Alleluia
Dedicated to Micaiah Lowe

Traditional
arranged by Gail Smith

Holy, Holy, Holy
Dedicated to Alex Hall

Reginald Heber

John B. Dykes
arranged by Gail Smith

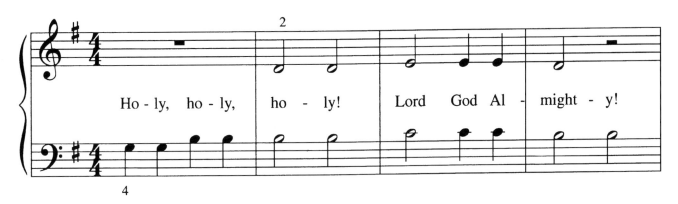

Ho - ly, ho - ly, ho - ly! Lord God Al - might - y!

Ear - ly in the morn - ing our song shall rise to Thee:

Ho - ly, ho - ly, ho - ly! Mer - ci - ful and might - y!

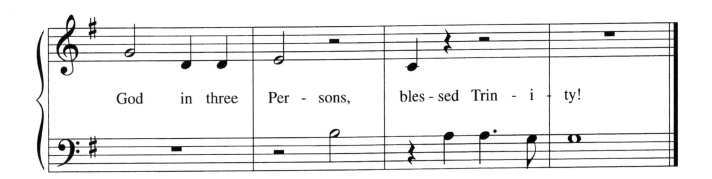

God in three Per - sons, bles - sed Trin - i - ty!

My Jesus, I Love Thee
Dedicated to Erika Hall

William Featherstone

A. J. Gordon
arranged by Gail Smith

14

Fairest Lord Jesus

Crusader's Hymn
arranged by Gail Smith

melody in the bass

Fair - est Lord Je - sus, rul - er of all na - ture. O Thou of God and man the Son; Thee will I cher - ish, Thee will I hon - or, Thou my soul's glo - ry, joy and crown.

Come, Thou Almighty King

Felice de Giardini
arranged by Gail Smith

A Mighty Fortress Is Our God

Martin Luther

Martin Luther
arranged by Gail Smith

My Faith Looks Up to Thee

Ray Palmer

Lowell Mason
arranged by Gail Smith

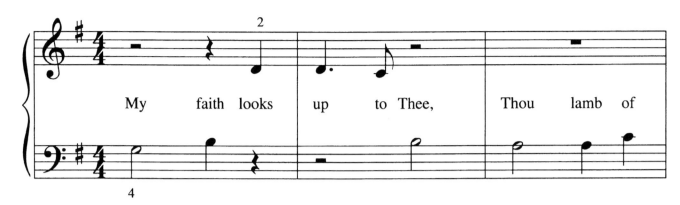

My faith looks up to Thee, Thou lamb of

Cal - va-ry, Sav - ior di - vine! Now hear me

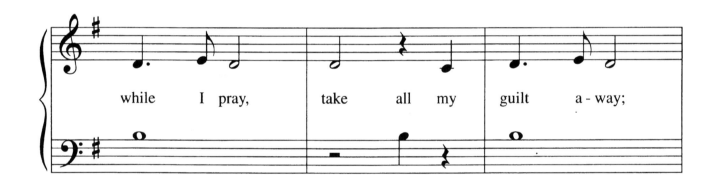

while I pray, take all my guilt a - way;

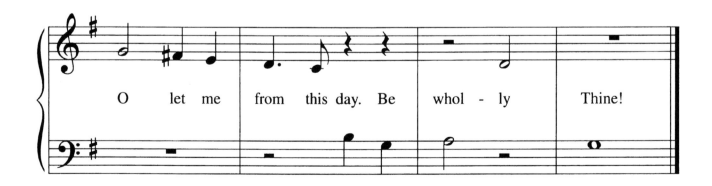

O let me from this day. Be whol - ly Thine!

Jesus, Keep Me Near the Cross

Fanny J. Crosby

William H. Doane
arranged by Gail Smith

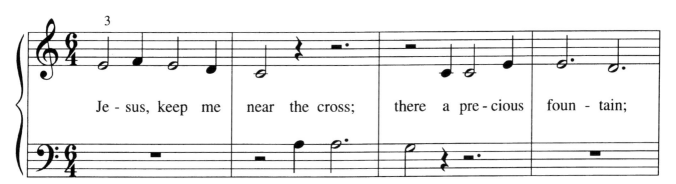

Je - sus, keep me near the cross; there a pre - cious foun - tain;

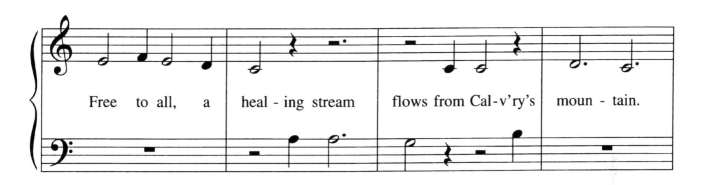

Free to all, a heal - ing stream flows from Cal-v'ry's moun - tain.

In the cross, in the cross, be my glo - ry ev - er.

'Till my rap - tured soul shall find rest, be-yond the ri - ver.

Crown Him with Many Crowns

Dedicated to Hannah Patten

Matthew Bridges

George J. Elvey
arranged by Gail Smith

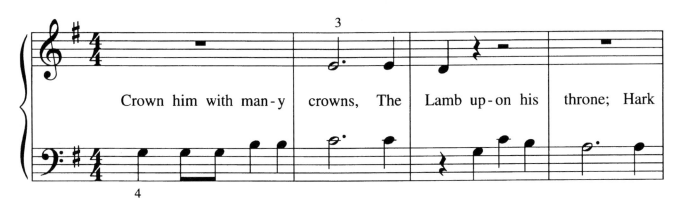

Crown him with man-y crowns, The Lamb up-on his throne; Hark

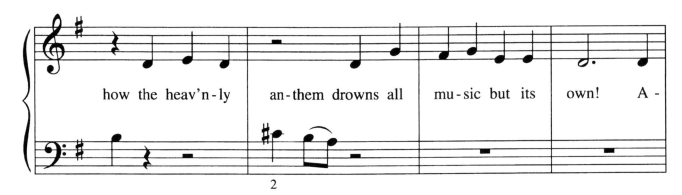

how the heav'n-ly an-them drowns all mu-sic but its own! A -

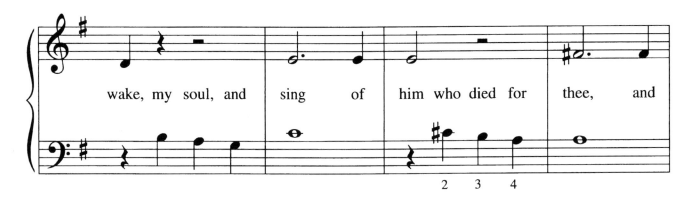

wake, my soul, and sing of him who died for thee, and

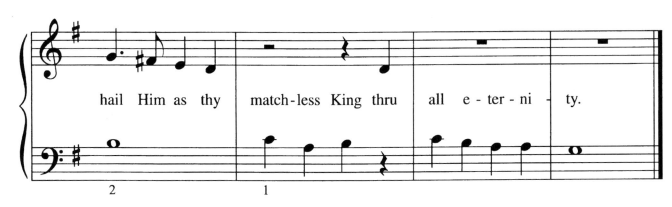

hail Him as thy match-less King thru all e-ter-ni-ty.

America the Beautiful

Katherine Bates

Samuel A. Ward
arranged by Gail Smith

Prayer for Protection

Dedicated to Joni Rosenthal

Gail Smith

Gail Smith

Gail Smith was born in Bridgeport, Connecticut, on January 26, 1943. Gail's father, Carl Erick Johnson, sang tenor in the church choir. Her mother, Ethel, played the piano and had Gail start piano lessons.

Smith received her Bachelor of Fine Arts Degree from Florida Atlantic University. She has taught piano students from the age of 3 to 96! Her blind student, Ivan, was seen on national TV. Giving musical lecture recitals by portraying the composer's wife has been an effective way to reach audiences with the history of music. Gail has portrayed Marian MacDowell and Anna Magdalena Bach. She gives many workshops and concerts throughout the United States as well as in Germany and Japan.

Smith's life has revolved around her family, church and music. She is the pianist of the famed Coral Ridge Presbyterian church. She has been active in many organizations including being national Music Chairman of the National League of American Pen Women and is a former president of the Broward County branch. Ms. Smith is also a member of The Freedoms Foundation of Valley Forge, National Music Teachers Association, and Federation of Music Clubs.

Ms. Smith's works include many piano solos, choral works, a piano trio, a composition for four pianos and numerous vocal solos. She has arranged hundreds of hymns, Indian melodies, and folk tunes from many countries. Her trademark is her piano palindromes, which can be played backwards as well as forwards and sound the same.

Printed in Great Britain
by Amazon